CHINESE ZODIAC SIGNS

CHINESE ZODIAC SIGNS

YEAR OF THE ROOSTER

 1909·1921·1933
1945·1957·1969
1981·1993·2005

ARROW

Arrow Books Limited
17-21 Conway Street, London W1P 6JD
An imprint of the Hutchinson Publishing Group
London Melbourne Sydney Auckland
Johannesburg and agencies throughout the world
First published by M.A. Editions 1982
Arrow edition 1984
© M.A. Editions 1982

Produced by Aurum Press, 33 Museum Street, London WC1
Original text in French by Catherine Aubier
Translated by Eileen Finletter and Ian Murray
Designed by Julie Francis
Phototypeset in Optima
by York House Typographic, Hanwell, London
Made and printed in Great Britain
by Anchor Brendon Limited, Tiptree, Essex

ISBN 0 09 933510 7

CONTENTS

In the same series

HOW TO USE THIS BOOK

Each section of this book gives a detailed description of the character, personality and partnership possibilities of the Rooster. The characteristics of this sign are described in conjunction with the important ascendant sign.

There is also a synthesis of the Chinese zodiac and the more familiar Western zodiac. Together these give new meaning and depth to the description and prediction of an individual's personality, the main tendencies of his character, his behaviour and the broad outline of his destiny.

The book concludes with the fascinating astrological game, the I Ching.

The arrangement of the book is as follows:

A short introduction to the background and philosophy of the Chinese zodiac (page 8).

A description of the characteristics of your specific Chinese sign, determined by the *year of your birth* — in this case the Rooster (page 19).

The best (and worst) partners for that Sign, determined by *the hour of your birth* (page 40).

The combination and interaction of your sign with the Ascendant Element: Earth, Water, Fire, Wood, Metal (page 49).

The comparison and combination of the two zodiacs — Chinese and Western (for example, the Sagittarian Rooster, the Virgo Rooster) — highlight many subtleties which enable you to clarify your psychological portrait (page 66).

The astrological game of the I Ching, which adapts the ancient Taoist 'Book of Mutations' to each Chinese sign. This simple game offers the reader the opportunity to obtain wise and appropriate answers to abstract as well as everyday questions (page 75).

THE MYSTERIES OF CHINESE ASTROLOGY

中國星相
學之神秘

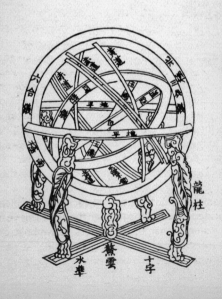

龍柱

水華   慧雲   十字

The legend of Buddha

One Chinese New Year more than five centuries before Christ, Buddha invited all the animals in creation to come to him, promising them recompense appropriate to his all-powerful and miraculous kindness and generosity. However, dimmed by their preoccupations of the moment (is it not said in the West that the characteristic of the animal is merely to eat, sleep, couple and fear?), almost all of them ignored the call of the Divine Sage. Yet twelve of the animals did go to him. They were, in order of their arrival, the Rat, Ox, Tiger, Rabbit, Dragon, Snake, Horse, Goat, Monkey, Rooster, Dog and Pig (other traditions replace the Rabbit with the Cat and the Pig with the Wild Boar).

To thank them Buddha offered each a year which would be dedicated to him alone through the ages. This year would carry the animal's name, and express his symbolic character and his specific psychological traits, marking the personality and behaviour of people born during that year.

Thus a cycle of twelve years was established, fitting exactly the sequence and rhythm of this improbable bestiary (one can imagine the dizzying amount of work which would have faced the astrologer if all of the animals had answered Buddha's invitation!).

Such is the legend.

The lunar cycle

Actually, Chinese astrology precedes the development of Far Eastern Buddhism, which began only in the 5th century of the Christian era, or about one thousand years after Buddha's appearance on earth. However, astrologers were already practising their art in China ten centuries before Christ; but the very origins of this astrology are as controversial as they are immemorial.

One point cannot be disputed: contrary to the West, which developed a solar astrology based on the apparent displacements of the daily star as its position in the Western zodiac changed from month to month, the Far East constructed a lunar astrology based on the annual cycle of lunar movements. This is why the Asian New Year — the Tet celebration among the Vietnamese — never falls exactly on the same date (page 93).

While the phases of the moon are equally important for a Western astrologer, their context is inscribed differently, with the result that their play of correspondence — and so their meanings and implications — are not comparable to those of Eastern astrology.

Without entering too deeply into scientific considerations which would lead us away from the purposes of this book, let us simply remind ourselves of the obvious and multiple influences of the moon, for example the movement of the tides, as well as more subtle levels, such as the female cycles and the obscure depths of the psyche. The term 'lunatic' has a precise and, indeed, clinical meaning. Recent statistical studies, for example, have made it possible to establish a strange and significant increase in acts of violence and criminality on nights when there is a full moon. Also, rigorous tests have established the direct impact of the moon on the chemical composition of certain bodies whose molecular structure can be modified depending on whether or not they have been exposed to lunar light.

Nuances of Chinese astrology

So, here we are with our twelve animals, the *Emblems* of Chinese astrology. Does this mean that all persons born in the same year as, say, the Rat or the Horse, will be subject to the same formulae of character and destiny? No more so than that those born under the sign of Aries or Libra are all confined to the same zodiacal script.

In Western astrology, the position of the planets, the calculation of the Ascendant and the Golden Mean of the Sky and its Mansions, allows the astrologer to refine and individualize a given theme considerably. In the same way, in Chinese astrology one obtains some surprisingly detailed and complex results. This is achieved by integrating with the intitial data factors such as the *Companion in Life* (determined by the hour of birth, but not to be confused with the Western Ascendant), and the predominant *Element*, which refers to the five Elements: Earth, Water, Fire, Wood and Metal.

This triple point of view — the *Emblematic Animal*, the *Companion in Life* and the *Element* — provide the reader with a greater diversity of references and a totality of perspectives both more rich and more precise than those found in Western astrology. To this we have added a detailed interpretation of the relationship between the Chinese and Western signs. The two astrologies are by nature distinct but never contradictory, and therefore complementary aspects and fusion can only result in a more profound understanding of the psychological types emanating from them. However, it is important to stress that although the concept of analogy holds an important place in Chinese astrology, it bears neither the same sense nor the same overall significance as in Western astrology.

Each Chinese sign is a universe in itself, a small cosmos with its own laws and domains, completely independent of all other signs. Each of these living creatures is given specific powers and functions, becoming an emblematic animal endowed with a particular dimension peculiar unto itself. It creates its own jungle or cavern, and defines by its rhythm its own cadences and breathing. In this way it secretes its own chemistry — or, rather, its own alchemy. It is a supple, mobile, fluctuating image, governed by its own internal metamorphoses and contradictions.

Once we understand this, we will see that it is fatal to impose a fixed framework or clearly circumscribed area of mental categories and psychological equations in order to protect or reassure an anguished ego seeking a comforting or flattering projection of its own desires and fears.

Our alignment to a Chinese sign cannot be defined by exclusive formulae or linear classifications. The Chinese symbol unfolds slowly, a gift of the Gods, of Time and of Mystery; a delectable or poisoned gift which an Oriental person accepts with humility because he knows that its flavour may be born of the poison, as its poison may be born of the flavour.

Sometimes, in the course of a lifetime, it is circumstances more than a character trait which seem to determine and crystallize the principal tendencies of a sign. In such cases a thread of major or minor events will tend to form a symphonic background to the style of, say, a Dragon or a Rat.

To Have and To Be

Through the centuries Chinese astrology has permeated and inspired the mental attitudes and behaviour of hundreds of millions of people in the Far East, to an extent that is difficult for us to accept or even appreciate.

To understand better the spirit in which these people rely on the art of contemplation in handling the problems of daily life, a cardinal point must be emphasized — one which probably constituted the essential and fundamental difference between Eastern and Western civilizations, and poses a virtually impassable dividing line between them.

In our Western 'consumer society' — irrespective of the admiring or negative feelings we may associate with this expression — the fundamental question, from birth to death and at all levels of activity, is: *'What can I have?'*. We are continuously asking what we might possess or enjoy; what material goods, fortune, luck, honours or power might be had; whether we will achieve success in love, prestige, a good job, family, health, home, friends or, on another level, culture and knowledge. It is always a question of, 'What can I obtain, preserve, enlarge?' which underlies the totality of our motivations.

Think of the *models* that are held up to us: the successful politicians, business tycoons, film and stage stars, celebrated artists or scientist, sports champions, heroes of crime novels or comic strips. Idols of all kinds incarnate the triumph and glory of 'to have'. All will say, 'I have the most power, the most money, the most diplomas and abilities', or even, 'Mine is the greatest love affair'. Or, why not 'Mine is the most terrible drama, the most frightful illness'? Esteem is won exclusively from what one *has*.

Still more obvious is advertising, which is omnipresent today, and proclaims that one must absolutely *have* such and such a product in order *to be:* dynamic, seductive, happy, at ease with oneself or wholly fulfilled.

For Orientals, the decisive question is not *'What can I have?'* but *'Whom can I be?'* The model aspired to is not the great leader, the hero or the champion, but the poor, naked Sage who has attained total freedom and perfect peace within himself. Princes and great businessmen bow low before him, for he is the image of the highest self-realization possible to man. In this perspective, the Sage renounces nothing; on the contrary, since he has attained the supreme reality, he is immeasurably richer than the most powerful ruler.

It is we who, due to our fragmented and illusory attachments, our infantile whims and our incessant conflicts, continually forgo the most marvellous felicity of all — God.

'Who am I?' Whatever approaches and methods, schools, sects or forms of asceticism are followed, this question, in appearance so simple and banal, lies at the base of and is the key to all Oriental culture. Through it lies the way to true liberation, by way of those roads to genuine understanding and knowledge known as Yoga, Vedanta, Tantra, Tao and Zen — to cite only the best known.

All this may cause the Chinese approach to astrology to seem disconcerting to us. The Oriental does not think 'I have such and such predispositions, aptitudes or weaknesses inherent in my horoscope', but rather, 'How can I be a Rat (or a Goat or a Dog) in all the circumstances of my life?'

The Oriental's goal is not 'to have' in the same way in which we in the West say 'I possess such and such a quality or defect'. For him, it is instead a question of directions, implying a subtle and rhythmic progression; a sort of poetic dance of destiny, with each animal possessing its own steps and pirouettes — an entire choreography of its own.

These subtleties must be perceived clearly by those who wish to evolve without losing their way or turning round in circles in this immense domain of shimmering and shifting aspects of understanding.

The astrological I Ching

In the last section of this book, we present a game inspired by the oracles of the I Ching and adapted to each sign.

In his book *Zen Buddhism*, Alan Watts wrote: 'The I Ching is a work of divination containing oracles based on 64 abstract figures, each composed of six traits. These traits are of two sorts: divided or negative and undivided or positive. A modern psychologist would recognize an analogy with the Rorschach test, whose aim is to establish the mental portrait of an individual according to the spontaneous images suggested to him by an inkspot or an over-elaborate design.

A subject whose images are inspired by the inkspot should be able to use his subsequent perceptions to deduce the necessary practical information to guide his future behaviour. Considered in this way, the divinatory art of the I Ching cannot be attacked as a vulgar superstition.'

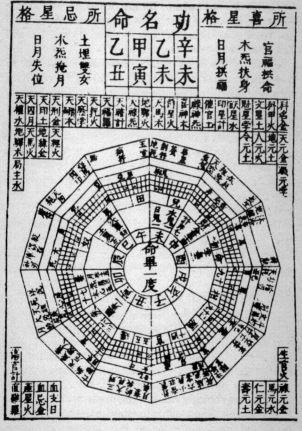

The relationship between the Signs and the Lunar Mansions

The practitioner of the I Ching commands an entire critical survey of the methods available when important decisions have to be made. We, on the other hand, are convinced that our decisions are rational because we depend upon a cluster of valid data affecting a problem; not for us to leave it to a mere game of heads or tails. The practitioner, however, might question whether we know what information is truly valid, given the fact that our plans are being constantly upset by events which are wholly unpredictable. Indeed, if we were rigorously rational in our choices of the data upon which our behaviour depended, so much time would be required that the moment for action would pass before we could assemble the data. Although we may set out initially to seek this information in a scientific manner, we are rapidly forced to act on another basis — capricious intuition, the impossibility of thinking further because we are too exhausted, or simply that time is too short and a choice must be made. In other words, our most important decisions are based largely on impressions, on our capacity to 'feel' a situation.

Every practitioner of the I Ching knows this. He is aware that his method is not an exact science but a useful and effective approach, if he is endowed with sufficient powers of intuition or, as he would say, 'in the Tao'.

THE YIN AND THE YANG

The *Yin* and the *Yang* are the symbols of two opposing and complementary principles whose indissoluble play and constant metamorphosis represent the roots, indeed the very tissues of the universe in action. They represent the eternal opposites — Positive-Negative, Yes-No, White-Black, Day-Night, Full-Empty, Active-Passive, Masculine-Feminine, and so on. Each contains within itself the germ of the other. That is why the man (Yang) bears within himself a feminine component (Yin), and the woman (Yin) a masculine one (Yang).

The Yin-Yang coupling is both indissoluble and changeable, each of the two terms being also its opposite and complementary term. This is expressed by the traditional figure:

At the moment when the Yang (white, active) is at its apogee — the bulging, enlarged part — the Yin (black, passive) imperceptibly takes its place — the tapering part — and vice versa.

The Yin and the Yang have no 'moral' character, neither is superior nor inferior to the other. Their antithesis is as necessary and as little in conflict as that of the left hand and the right hand striking together to applaud.

THE YIN AND THE YANG TYPES

The Rat, Ox, Rabbit, Monkey, Dog and Pig are **Yin**.
The Tiger, Horse, Dragon, Snake, Goat and Rooster are **Yang**.

The Yin man

Appearance: The Yin man is often corpulent, of medium height and muscularly well developed. He is physically resilient to a marked degree and his health is sound. He often has a round face and does not smile much.

Psychology: The Yin man is above all self-preoccupied and inclined to consider himself the centre of the universe. Though his behaviour appears calm, his moods are unstable and susceptible to his immediate environment. He has great confidence in himself, yet fears failure. Sociable, hospitable, he is optimistic vis-à-vis himself and others. His life is active; he is pragmatic and efficient.

The Yang man

Appearance: He is of average weight, often tall and slender, even willowy. His face is smiling and he prefers strong colours. Of delicate health, he should be advised to prevent rather than wait to cure illness.

Psychology: The Yang man is an individualist and attracted to introspective meditation. He is intelligent, independent and at times solitary. He prefers his own company and communing with nature to living with the crowd. Contrary to the Yin man, he seeks his equilibrium within himself instead of finding it amongst others.

THE DOMAINS
OF
THE ROOSTER

十二生肖

THE ROOSTER
AND ITS SYMBOLISM

When one thinks of the Rooster, one symbol that comes to mind is the Gallic cock. However, this particular Rooster is a completely recent notion and possesses no mythological foundation, being only the warriorlike expression of an animal that represents the pride, daring and vigilance of the French soldier. Nevertheless, the Rooster found on the tops of monuments commemorating the dead has a tendency to evoke a creature of death and devastation and the memory and suffering of millions of men fallen in battle for their country.

The Rooster is above all a solar symbol, announcing the sun's rising with his morning song. In India he personifies solar energy; in Japan he incarnates the first manifestation of light; and in China he is designated by the character K, symbolizing the five virtues. He is a Rooster of good omen, favourable in his aspect and bearing, with his cockscomb giving him an air of authority. The way he carries his spurs symbolizes military virtue, the courage displayed during battles and his goodness, for the Rooster shares his food. Finally, he portrays confidence because of the assurance with which he greets the sunrise. All of which runs contrary to the aggressive and swaggering bird of popular imagery.

The Rooster is also the emblem of the hero and of the guardian and protector of life: is he not often at the top of buildings? Surmounting a weather vane, or roof, the Rooster is on the watch, looking down on men and scanning the horizon. In announcing the break of day he disperses ghosts and phantoms, the powers of illusion and darkness. He is the incarnation of the forces of youth, hope and clarity.

The following is from a 19th-century history of animals for young people and reflects the admiration with which the Rooster has been regarded for many centuries and in all civilizations:

'Rooster of proud bearing and sober walk, of a bold and

courageous character, Rooster distinguished by the fine lines of your body, by your plump blazing red crest, by the richness and the variety of your feathers, as well as by the agreeable contour of your tail feathers, your song is the clock of our countrysides, night and day. You are kind, obliging and attentive to your hens; you warn them of danger, call them to share with you your good fortune, generous to the point of foolishness. Alas, you are extremely jealous, and will suffer no rival. If your song is imitated, you become uneasy and alarmed, assemble your hens, protecting them assiduously. If you should fight another, you will do so courageously and until death rather than survive a shameful defeat . . . Sentinel, protector and guardian, you can be as dangerous and as wily as the worst rogue when it comes to protecting your own.'

With his mixture of conformity and eccentricity, aggressive impulses and meditative leanings, the Rooster is a rather strange and paradoxical animal. This captive king is a bizarre and contradictory creature, a ruler and a slave whose bravery and despotism are confined by the narrow limits of the farmyard. In this sense the Rooster is an analogy for the frailties of prestige and power, confined within the inevitable enclosure of time and death.

A few notes on the Rooster

Principal qualities: Honest, frank, obliging, courageous.
Principal defects: Vain, thoughtless, preoccupied with his appearance.
Work: Gives of himself completely. Tradition has it that he would find an earthworm in the desert.
Best role: Military hero or comic figure.
Worst role: Spy (he is too conspicuous).
Money: Very extravagant; he cannot resist temptation. His bank account often will be in the red.
Luck: He does not have much. All his life he will be forced to scratch the earth to find food. But if he is born in spring, he will be less of a braggart.

Cannot live without: Seducing. Admiring looks from others are a drug to him, even though he might not admit it.

Adores: From time to time to spend quiet holidays in an isolated and comfortable place.

Hates: Any attempt to probe his private being or expose his motives. In short, any attempt to lift his feathers to look underneath.

Leisure activities: Evenings spent socializing or reading.

Favourite places: He likes to have a corner of his own, decorated by him, where others can only enter by invitation. A kind of 'secret garden'.

Colour: Yellow.

Plants: Gentian; orange and palm trees.

Flowers: Sunflower, hawthorn.

Professions: Any commercial profession from salesman to sales director or sales representative; military officer; restaurant owner, hairdresser, public relations, farmer, aesthete, manicurist, teacher — and village cock!

The four ages in the life of the Rooster according to Chinese tradition

During his *childhood*, *youth* and *maturity*, the Rooster will often have problems and his life will be strewn with ups and downs. He will know the greatest joys and suffer the greatest sorrows; sometimes he will be rich, sometimes poor; sometimes he will be surrounded by friends, sometimes alone. But as soon as he attains emotional stability and becomes settled in a profession, his life will become calm. In any case, he will enjoy a happy *old* age.

THE PSYCHOLOGY OF THE ROOSTER

The personality of those born under the sign of the Rooster consists of three levels: *appearance*, *reality* and *emotion*. The first is so blinding that it often prevents us from the reaching the second, let alone the third.

According to tradition, Roosters are much above the common run of men. When one observes them — or rather when one has them before one's eyes, for they are hard to miss — one is struck first by their elegant gestures and rich colours. They are generally well-dressed, sometimes a bit ostentatiously. They like people to turn to look at them and they rarely pass unnoticed; their presence is unavoidable. Even a young Rooster wearing the strangest rags or patched blue jeans always leaves behind a half-admiring and half-irritated audience. Is it their aura? Their charm? This is hard to know.

These animals, whose role it is to announce the dawn, do not wish to be seen carelessly dressed. Some, more arrogant, even seem to think that the rising sun is simply obeying their cry. Scrupulous about their appearance, they become ruffled before others' lack of taste, and are never completely satisfied with their own warbling or plumage, even though they may seem to be sure of themselves.

Agreeable in society, easy and relaxed, wherever they may mingle, Roosters will be met with a cordial smile, be it in Buckingham Palace or a sitting room in a semi-detached in the suburbs. In either case, the hostess will find them charming and invite them back, which is why Roosters have a rather active social life.

Roosters are highly cultivated, and, beneath their light manner, are capable of serious conversation. Having read a great deal, they are knowledgeable and up-to-date on everything and possess an excellent memory. Yet, curiously, they rarely display their knowledge — as though they prefer to be judged by their famous feathers. Their crowning is an aspect of the second level, which we shall now look into.

Roosters only reveal themselves to their family and intimate friends, for they abhor being used as fodder for social conversations or as guinea pigs for amateur psychologists. Sooner or later one begins to question whether their superficiality is real or a game. The answer is that they conceal their inner selves with near desperation, obstinately camouflaging their lack of self-confidence and the fact that, at bottom, they are only fragile birds. What remains of a Rooster when one takes away his feathers and his cock-a-doodle-do? It is up to you to find out — he will not want to know.

Roosters are charming but sometimes difficult to live with, for they are very egocentric and completely preoccupied with their own needs, desires and longings. They serve themselves first — in all senses of the word — with total innocence and touching good faith. At table, if you are shocked to see them take the best morsels, they will reply angelically 'But it is only to see if it is good'.

Completely indifferent to the state of mind of others, they follow their own little route. In daily life they hate others to interfere in their affairs — and avoid interfering in those of others. If you pull at their feathers to tell them about a clogged sink or your baby having the measles, they will send you packing very brusquely indeed.

However, then comes the miracle which often makes these Roosters so adorable and appreciated — and with good reason. At the very moment when you hold in your arms your smallest child who is suffering from the flu, and your house has been flooded by a burst pipe, the Rooster will appear, stethoscope in one hand and plumbing tools in the other. With a charming smile he will arrange everything in a matter of minutes: your child will be sleeping peacefully, having been given the proper medicine, and your pipe will be mended. Roosters are extremely pleasant and obliging, especially in times of dire necessity. They love to be asked for help but do not like being asked direct questions about themselves.

Their greatest qualities are their honesty and frankness. Actually, they sometimes go too far! They say what they think with the delicacy of a bulldozer. They do not mean to hurt anyone's feelings, they simply think that it is helpful for you to know that your pudding is inedible or that your new hair style is a disaster. Mrs Rooster is even more guilty of this than the male, although she is almost always forgiven because everyone knows that she is not naturally malicious. So, although friendly, generous and charitable, Roosters cannot be counted on to be careful of the feelings of others. It is best to understand this from the start.

While loyal, sincere and capable of giving sensible advice, Roosters do not like to confide in others and prefer to solve their problems on their own. Their relationships thus lack give-and-take and confidence. Decidedly independent, they refuse to owe anything to anyone.

Roosters often seem original, even slightly eccentric, but at heart they are rather conforming. Although their rhythm of life is often unstable, their morality is as solid as a rock. They also give the impression of being adventurous, but in fact prize security, their home and their family. Yet in times of danger they are the most courageous and heroic persons in the Chinese zodiac.

As for the third level, we shall speak of their sensitivity, which is well hidden, even from themselves. Roosters fear their vulnerability, and, lest they be discovered, are distrustful and hide what they are feeling, preferring to appear insensitive. Most of the time they succeed, and are unhappy because of it. Sharing life with a Rooster is exciting, but not simple. They are gay, amusing, always ready for adventure and to discuss things. Understanding and available, and never appearing to be bored in your company, they often fall silent for a moment and then joke and change the subject. Be careful: although not on purpose, you have touched upon their secret garden. Perhaps one day they will open the door to you, but it is they who will choose the moment. If you try to force an entrance, you will only find a void, for if a Rooster does not wish to reveal something, he will make it invisible.

THE ROOSTER AS A CHILD

The young Rooster is alert, open and full of vivacity. Everything interests him, and, like his animal sign, he has a tendency to peck about from right to left, trying everything and spreading himself widely. Naturally gifted for many things, intelligent and curious, he likes to learn but has difficulty choosing. He often becomes passionate about a subject, takes a great deal of trouble to become knowledgeable about all aspects of it, and then becomes totally disinterested and passes on to something else with the same enthusiasm and intensity.

This 'touching on everything' side of the young Rooster deserves to be encouraged, for the knowledge he acquires might be useful later on. But the parents of a Rooster child must guide him in his choice of profession, which is not always simple for his capacities are extremely varied and, should he feel imprisoned in a field he finds dry and unrewarding, he will rebel and become discouraged. Invite your Rooster child to share your interests, open new horizons for him and travel with him — discovering new things enchants him. Encourage his hobbies, but do not become too excited if he reveals himself to be exceptionally gifted in something bizarre, since his enthusiasm may well be short-lived.

Try to prepare him for a reasonable and stable profession and encourage him to persevere; he appreciates comfort and security and from a young age will respond to your practical arguments. Persuade him to earn a diploma or degree; with this in hand he can afford to sow his wild oats. The important thing is that he plan for his future and that his impractical tendencies are held in check.

Rooster children are charming, easy to live with and, whether boys or girls, often daredevils. They need to be independent: avoid asking too many questions and respect their secrets.

Although capable of adapting to a slightly rigid educational system, the Rooster cannot bear injustice: the sight of it can turn him into an absolute rebel. On the other hand he is always particularly nice with his brothers and sisters, and, as an elder brother or sister, he is ideal. He dislikes solitude and will blossom more readily in the centre of a large family, where he will delightedly play the role of the little chieftain, and will assist in educating the others, for he is a very well-organized child.

LOVE LIFE

Neither Mr nor Mrs Rooster lack charm and both are precocious. In adolescence, the young female Rooster trails a crowd of admirers behind her, whom she leads by the nose. There is no need to worry about her future, for she is reasonable and will almost always choose someone who is at the very least acceptable, or even brilliant, but in any case well able to support a family. She will adapt to married life with wisdom and humour. Mrs Rooster is sociable, communicative and very active. If she is a housewife, there is no doubt that she will be perfect; otherwise she will not care a fig about housework and will devote herself to her career. She is frank and honest, agreeable and gay, never conceals anything and will be faithful to her duty and true to her promises. She can be carried away by passion, but will never lose her footing or her head, for beneath a sometimes carefree and frivolous appearance, she has a keen sense of her responsibilities.

Mr Rooster is often a swaggering braggart. When young he collects conquests, rapidly discarding those who give in too quickly, for difficulty attracts and inspires him. He likes to have an entire hen house, with a well-organized hierarchy, at his disposal. Like a sultan and his harem, he will have 'favourite' and 'regular' girlfriends — and others kept in reserve. His fidelity is completely relative. Certainly he is faithful, but to several women at a time.

Roosters are not always easy to live with for they jealously protect their independence and refuse to allow interference. Tradition has it that they make better friends than lovers because their off-hand manner and sometimes outrageous frankness causes those who love them to suffer.

They are, however, jealous, and this is true of both the males and females. They hate to be supplanted by a rival, but take care not to show it for they dislike displaying their deeper emotions. They are often mistakenly thought to be indifferent.

One piece of advice if you are in love with a Rooster: do not overwhelm him or her with devouring passion nor insist on conversation. They adore long philosophic discussions, provided they are not personally nor directly involved. They are extremely sensual and greedy on all levels.

FAMILY LIFE

Although relaxed and whimsical in appearance, Roosters are aware of their familial responsibilities, and when they have made a commitment on this level, they keep it. At bottom they are conformists, endowed with an impeccable moral sense, and respect conventions from the moment they choose family life. They can live the joyously irregular life of a dashing bachelor and then change to a married life that is perfectly peaceful and well-organized.

They are usually against divorce and try to avoid it — but if there is a total breakdown of understanding, they will accept it, for they are too frank to live hypocritically.

Roosters are firm yet warm parents, and their children will never want for anything. However, the children, especially if they are sensitive, could suffer from the independence of their Rooster parents, who egotistically, will rarely sacrifice their personal pleasures for the needs of their offspring. This is unconscious on the Roosters' part; they have clear consciences and hardly ever suffer from guilt. Their aim is to give their family the essentials — but no more. On the other hand, if a family member is in trouble or if the family security is threatened, they become generous, courageous and will not lose their heads, whatever difficulties they must contend with.

Rat, Rabbit or Dog children — who have a need to be pampered — will feel misunderstood and resent their

Rooster parent. Ox, Goat and Pig children will submit to discipline without too much difficulty. But there will be trouble with Tigers, Dragons and Horses, all of whom will systematically refuse to bend to the will of the Rooster, who will consequently often lose some of his feathers. Monkey and Snake children will reap many rewards from their Rooster parent, for communication will be open and continuous. The rest will have to rely on being philosophic.

PROFESSIONAL LIFE

Roosters can succeed in all professions that demand self-assurance, nerve and brilliance. Intelligent and skilful, they know how to convince and persuade others. Their taste for comfort and security encourages their desire for a good salary and their appreciation of efficiency and practicality, but they dislike routine, and prefer independence to subordinate positions.

This is why Roosters do so well in the acting profession, where they can behave like strutting peacocks; and in positions which involve travelling and in which their qualities will be recognized.

Roosters generally prefer to impose their own self-discipline rather than submit to outside demands, but they are conscientious. They are reasonably ambitious, yet prefer to become department heads and maintain their sanity, rather than managing directors and risk a heart attack. Thanks to a harmonious mixture of perseverence, frankness and energy, they rise easily in the social scale. They are both appreciated and feared for their stony sincerity and their systematic refusal to take catastrophies seriously — at least in appearance; their smile is their best weapon, but there are occasions when it is uncalled for.

Many Roosters have an unstable working life, changing jobs according to their dreams and not worrying too much about the future. Only the dependence of their family will have a truly stabilizing effect on them, and only their moral responsibilities to their family will keep them from being short-sighted and unreasonable. Unlike Rabbits, they face extreme situations more easily than small obstacles. Impressionable beneath their cool and sure exterior, they sometimes get lost in details, forgetting the essentials. It is useless to intervene: they prefer to handle their problems on their own.

In their work they are highly organized, even meticulous, and become furious when someone moves their papers; but they are enthusiastic and face difficulties with a smiling courage that is unequalled in the Chinese zodiac. They are quite dashing!

MATERIAL LIFE

If you are married to a Rooster, one piece of advice: earn your own money and keep your own accounts because Roosters are incapable of organizing a budget and are real spendthrifts. They simply love to spend money, first on themselves (believing that charity begins at home) and then on their families. The only exceptions are those Roosters who suffered from poverty in their early lives.

Paradoxically, Roosters can be extremely stingy if out with friends whom they consider able to pay. If you invite Mrs Rooster to dinner because you find her attractive, do not expect her to offer to share the bill; but with girlfriends, she will be spontaneous and generous. Roosters' bank accounts are often in the red, or about to become so. This, however, does not bother them very much. Financial power does not interest them in the least: they only want to satisfy their needs and not have to deprive themselves. The hoarders among the Rats or Ox's would do well to imitate this healthy philosophy. Whether a Rooster must be careful of what he spends, or whether he spends without thinking of tomorrow, he has the same relaxed attitude. Roosters possess the wisdom to take life as it comes.

ENVIRONMENT

It is not uncommon for a Rooster to claim that he can sleep anywhere, adapt himself to any climate and dress in any old way. However, in his daily life he is likely to take at least two showers a day, and spend a great part of his free time buying new gadgets for his home in order to make it more comfortable.

He is a good example of the ambivalence of those born under this sign: capable of having the wildest fantasies on holiday, he will be maniacal and finicky at home. A Rooster's home is harmonious and comfortable, with simple but expensive objects, soft sofas and well-organized cupboards.

It must not be forgotten, however, that Roosters are adaptable, which helps them to feel fine anywhere. They are sensitive to anything pretty or agreeable, are smiling and at ease, and are able to create a special universe around themselves. They rarely feel out of their element, except when faced with ostentation or filth. If you lack imagination or the taste for interior decorating, ask a Rooster friend over — he will change your objects around, move the furniture and help you choose or change your colour scheme.

A guide to relations with a Rooster
Methods of seduction:

He: Courts you in three stages. He puts everything into the first stage — amazing, stunning, impressing and exciting you. In the second stage he will try to make himself indispensable to you. And finally, the third stage — must be censored.

She: Is flirtatious and has a free and easy manner. You may think that you are the one and only, but beware! In any case, you will have to show your credentials — and they had better be impressive — before she makes up her mind.

If he loves you: There will be great romantic moments in the style of 'I never thought such complete understanding to be possible'. Take care, however, that you share interests and responsibilities. Be exceptional, or you will find yourself imprisoned in a hen-house and lost in the crowd, for the Rooster is not faithful by nature and quickly resumes his old habits.

He expects of you: That you be his accomplice and that you speak or remain silent depending on his mood. This requires some training.

To keep you: He will make as few concessions as possible — just enough to keep you from throwing a plate at him.

If he is unfaithful: He will be very lordly indeed, and she will play the great lady: 'But, have you forgotten? I told you that you were perfectly free to do as you wished.'

In case of a break between you: He, or she, will remain a faithful friend and will not hold a grudge.

If you wish to give him a gift: It is the feeling that counts, so you can buy clothes or anything for the house and not make an embarrassing mistake. Not something too expensive, because then he will feel obliged to do the same and may dislike this. Think of the gift as merely a gesture — something bought on a trip, for example, which you can tell him cost practically nothing; he will be comfortable and happy that you thought of him.

If you want to seduce him: Tell him not only how handsome he is, but how intelligent and profound!

If you want to get rid of him: Suggest sweetly that it might be a good idea to see a psychoanalyst!

THE ROOSTER AND THE OTHER CHINESE SIGNS

Rooster/Rat

One always fears that the Rat sees only the defects of the Rooster and becomes hypnotized by them. Then and there he will refuse to engage with this individual, so horribly sure of himself, and will pronouce him vain and superficial.

If the Rat takes the trouble to delve beneath appearances, he will discover qualities in the Rooster which please him. Once they get together, they will merrily criticize their circle of friends and acquaintances.

On the other hand, if they should turn their aggressions and their critical capacities against each other, a real boxing match will develop. Then, too, neither of them has any idea of economy. They would become broke and ruin each other in no time, at first with gifts and then with lawsuits.

A combination of a male Rat and female Rooster works better, because the female Rooster is level-headed and knows how to handle day-to-day life, even though it irritates her. If it is the Rat who is female, they will do well to open a shop for cut-rate goods, hire an amiable sales-girl and contrive not to eat up all their capital.

Rooster/Ox
No problems here! The Ox will allow the Rooster to shine in peace, and will be aware of the useful and important role that a sociable spouse can play in his life, since he is so often accused of being too grave and taciturn. Both need freedom, and therefore easily understand each other's need for it. The Rooster likes to sing in peace, and will willingly leave the Ox to organize their daily life. Also, despite his flamboyant nature, the Rooster has a conformist and reasonable side. It is in these latter aspects that he will find most harmony with his Ox spouse.

Obviously, sometimes there will be friction. For example when Mr Rooster unexpectedly brings home a whole carload of friends for dinner; or when the Ox — male or female — sharply criticizes the Rooster in front of friends.

At work the Ox and the Rooster will get along in a highly profitable way. But it must be the Ox who manages the enterprise, while the Rooster takes care of public relations.

Rooster/Tiger
Here, good understanding will not be easy. Although sensitive and loyal, the Tiger is not noted for his reflective abilities. He is neither subtle nor discerning; he judges others by their behaviour, their acts, and even by their reputations. It is their appearance which counts, not their spiritual meanderings. But the Rooster cannot be judged solely by his appearance: it is too elaborate and too brilliant, and one could easily believe that nothing lies behind it.

In the beginning, everything will go well. The Tiger will be flattered by the personality of his fine-feathered Rooster, while the latter will sincerely admire the Tiger's courage. Very quickly, however, the little boasts of the Rooster will irritate his companion, who will not hesitate to criticize. No Rooster can tolerate being constantly reproved, and he will feel himself misunderstood and treated unjustly. He will rapidly set out to seek a more indulgent companion, but, before leaving, he will tell the Tiger a few home truths; he values his reputation for frankness.

These two can be associates, friends or even lovers, but not for long. Essentially, they are not at all on the same wave-length.

Rooster/Rabbit

Whether their relationship is based on friendship, love or professional ties, this duo often risks ending in a fist fight. In fact, no Rabbit has the patience needed to endure the swaggerings and boastings of the Rooster, who often exaggerates — most of the time without reason — just to amuse himself or to see how people react.

The usually patient and peaceful Rabbit will watch his tolerance evaporate quickly. The Rooster makes him literally boil, and our Rabbit cannot stop himself from wanting to snatch at some of the Rooster's feathers in order to diminish his vanity. The Rooster, who actually has no bad intentions, will see the Rabbit's attitude as one of malice — and he will not be entirely wrong.

If the Rabbit is the male, he will seek to confine Mrs Rooster to a role of submissive housekeeper, she, in turn will take advantage of his first absence to fly out the window. If the Rooster is the male, his Rabbit wife will criticize him ceaselessly, which he will not understand.

Rooster/Dragon

They both like to shine, but in totally different ways. The Rooster seeks to please because it reassures him of his personal value; the Dragon dazzles because he is naturally like that.

With these two, everything can go very well indeed. The Rooster will know how to fan the Dragon's flames as their warmth envelops him. He will admire the Dragon, who need make no effort to be seductive, and will be proud of having captured his attention. The adulated Dragon in turn will feel like a proud peacock and will be happy indeed. Danger will come in moments of crisis or misunderstanding, which, alas, can be frequent. The Dragon has little awareness of subtleties and no psychological understanding whatsoever; sometimes he will be tough and intolerant with his Rooster companion, who will then wish to take him down a peg or two.

Rooster/Snake
This is the ideal couple of Chinese astrology. Traditionally they represent mind and matter, balancing themselves in harmonious union. They get along marvellously together. From the start they will appreciate each other's elegance: they could even buy matching outfits and look like fashion photographs. They love each other for their flattering appearance as a couple; even more, they understand each other perfectly. The Rooster will be able to sing in peace, and, between cock-a-doodle-do's, will recount his exploits to the Snake, who will comment on them with wit and humour. The Snake will feel secure because of the hard-working side of the farm-yard king, who will finally feel understood, being accepted as he is and not judged only by his brilliant plumage.

The Rooster and the Snake are accomplices. Even if they argue — usually because of an infidelity — their dialogue will always bring them together; they adore philosophizing into the small hours of the morning.

Rooster/Horse
This combination is far from ideal: each needs to have his or

her true value recognized and affirmed; appearance is important to them; they are sensitive to the opinion of others — particularly the Horse — and both are very vulnerable. You may think that they thus have many points in common. But in fact they have too many, and both will try to take first place and rank ahead of the other. All the love in the world cannot overcome this reflex.

Also, these similarities do not lead to evolution, but to irritation. The Horse will suffer at seeing his Rooster partner strut about, and will have neither the patience nor the wisdom to allow him to crow in peace. For his part, the Rooster will be dissatisfied because he needs dialogue, and discussion with a Horse is often limited to agreeing that he is right.

Rooster/Goat
They do not have much in common except, perhaps, a love of the countryside and a certain flair for socializing. They do not really understand each other. The Goat will feel secure, for the Rooster will work for two, but he will expect in return understanding, permanent companionship and a form of encouragement amounting to moral support which the Goat will be unable to provide.

Although he may pretend to be unconcerned, the Rooster will be deeply upset and will withdraw into himself, a role at which he is a specialist. The Goat, assuming the truth to be revealed by the role, will retreat within his vagabond spirit — and the rift between the two will continue to widen.

If the man is a Goat and the woman a Rooster, she will nag him ceaselessly and will not tolerate his 'bohemian' side. But if she can be his manager, she will be excellent and do great things for him. In this way they will reach a better understanding and the mutual respect they gain will cement their alliance.

Rooster/Monkey
This alliance can work, but only superficially. While the

astute, clever Monkey and the honest, frank Rooster complete each other, the former will always have a tendency to mock, criticize and treat the Rooster as a superficial, naive person. The Rooster, on the other hand, will for a while admire the acrobatic games of his partner, but will end by saying: 'Ah, I didn't realize that he was so superficial!'

By judging each other solely on external appearances, they will methodically detect the mote in their companion's eye and not the dust in their own.

Their problem is that they cannot accept that they are on an equal footing, and so they live at war with each other as perpetual rivals. However, a little indulgence and acceptance of the other 'as he is', without wishing to change him, would enable this couple to live in comparative peace.

They can agree on one level: their mutual taste for parties and social life. They will squabble ceaselessly, but what a handsome couple they make!

Rooster/Rooster

This relationship is rather lively. They are either extremely fond of each other, but squabble a lot — or they do not like each other at all, and do not mind saying so. Those who have difficulty accepting their own faults are usually incapable of accepting them in others; without realizing it these Roosters get on their high horses and a cock fight will quickly ensue.

This mini-war is of no great importance between a man and a woman, but it can become quite dumbfounding between the same sex. A valuable alliance can only really exist between parents and children whose apparant contempt hides a secret esteem, which, curiously, usually occurs between two Roosters.

Rooster/Dog

These two signs share a common attribute: a critical mentality. The Rooster manifests this in a rather systematic way — sometimes criticizing simply to talk, sometimes to be interesting and at others just to make people laugh — but he never considers the wounds he is inflicting in the process. The Dog will be critical deliberately and consciously, particularly when his nerves are on edge, as they are by the typical defects of the Rooster — his boasting, bragging side; his constant use of 'me' and 'I'; his ease and freedom from care. Given his anxieties, this seems personally injurious to the Dog. So their relationship easily degenerates into a war of words. Each will suffer, for both are sensitive.

However, if they can control themselves and hold their tongues — if one rejects a taste for the tough, hurtful remark and the other his moral rigidity — they could really help each other; for their qualities are complementary. But will they make the necessary effort?

Rooster/Pig

Everything is possible with the tolerant Pig, who has a thick skin and is not excessively disturbed by the pricks of the Rooster. He is even one of those rare persons who can recognize the Rooster's goodness and kindness which lie hidden beneath his brilliant feathers. The Pig disarms the Rooster's aggressiveness, understands him and tranquillizes him.

However, the Rooster will never try to take advantage of the Pig. They get along very well together, although their relationship will be one of comradeship rather than passionate love or intellectual stimulation. They will take life easily, but will be ready to fly to help each other at the least sign of danger. What could be better? A little spice perhaps, for the unforeseen, the delicious surprise, will often be lacking with these two.

SOME ROOSTER CELEBRITIES

Alexander I and Catherine II of Russia, Colette, Fenimore Cooper, Copernicus, William Faulkner, Fulton, Goebbels, Kierkegaard, La Fontaine, Marie Laurencin, Andre Maurois, Marie de Medici, Princess Caroline of Monaco, Yves Montand, Patton, Madame Recamier, Richelieu, Johann Strauss, Strindberg, Telemann, Verdi, Queen Victoria, Wagner.

YOUR COMPANION IN LIFE

生命伴侣

After the Chinese sign of your year of birth, here is the sign of your hour of birth

What is a Companion in Life, as understood in Chinese astrology? It is a sort of 'ascendant' sign corresponding to your hour of birth. This Companion is another animal belonging to the Chinese cycle of the twelve emblematic beasts, who falls into step with you and accompanies you, ever ready to help you brave the traps and ambushes along your route. A permanent and benevolent shadow, he can render the impossible possible.

He is your counterpart, but with his own character and tendencies and with a different psychology. Both guardian angel and devil's advocate, he will be a witness to your life and an actor in it.

Have you ever felt, deep inside yourself, the subtle presence of another 'myself' inhabiting you and with whom you live, at times in harmony, at others in conflict? Another self who sometimes criticizes you and at others encourages you? That is your Companion in Life.

There are times when he will appear to be an imposter or an intruder. Certainly, he often questions your habits and your moral or spiritual complacency. Accompanied by this companion, a shadow within, the route is less monotonous and the voyager multiplies his chances of arriving at his chosen destination. This, however, in itself matters little, for it is the journey and the manner in which it is conducted that are important. Indolence is the greatest danger: your Companion is capable of arousing you from a lassitude of spirit and, to that end, if necessary, robbing you of your certainties, trampling on your secret gardens and, finally, tearing away the great veil of illusion.

It sometimes happens that your Companion is of the same sign as your year of birth, a twin brother in a way — for example, a Rooster/Rooster. In this case, you must recognize that he will compel you to realize yourself fully and to live the double aspect — the Yin and the Yang — that your bear within yourself. In any case, you also bear within yourself the twelve animals. So, set out on the long route, ready for the great adventure: the beautiful voyage during which you will encounter the harmoniously entangled, the solemn and the grotesque, the ephemeral reality, the dream and the imagined.

Table of hours corresponding to the twelve emblematic animals

If you were **born** between	your **companion** is
11 pm and 1 am	Rat
1 am and 3 am	Ox
3 am and 5 am	Tiger
5 am and 7 am	Rabbit
7 am and 9 am	Dragon
9 am and 11 am	Snake
11 am and 1 pm	Horse
1 pm and 3 pm	Goat
3 pm and 5 pm	Monkey
5 pm and 7 pm	Rooster
7 pm and 9 pm	Dog
9 pm and 11 pm	Pig

These figures correspond to the *solar hour* of your birth. If necessary, you should check the summer times (Daylight Savings Time) and make the appropriate adjustment (sometimes two hours before or after statutory time).

THE ROOSTER AND ITS COMPANION IN LIFE

Rooster/Rat

The Rooster, announcing the rising of the sun, and the Rat, busy with his nocturnal activities, are two companions who will hardly have time for sleep. For these two dissimilar characters, a true understanding may seem impossible, yet it is precisely in this that they may prove to be complementary to each other. The Rooster will perch; the Rat will burrow. Each has a lively nature. The one is a sun symbol, the other a symbol of night. They will mutually strengthen each other. Rat will offer his world of the underground on a gold platter to the Rooster at the very moment when the Rooster, ruffling his feathers, is rising on his spurs awaiting the moment of dawn's song. This is a daily offering on which the Rat would do well to meditate. For Master Rat, so often taking but rarely giving, this generous Rooster will be a source of strength, if he knows how to take what is offered.

Rooster/Ox

The Rooster will add a little wine to his water, or, more exactly, he will add a pinch of generosity to his egotism. The Rooster has a sense for sharing and for friendship; admittedly he can behave like a braggart, but then his very ardour and vivacity are so charming that one forgives him everything. From his bravado the Ox will gain a great deal. The morning song of the Rooster will relieve the Ox of a certain torpor and dullness. The ideal would be composed of the Rooster's sharpness on the surface and the Ox's ability in depth.

Rooster/Tiger

He detests banality. His creed is based on the need to be first and to dominate. He is unequalled where the question of pride is concerned; be careful, a voyage is always beset with traps and surprises. The Tiger/Rooster will have a tendency to believe himself to be the winner every time. Alas, the higher he climbs, the greater the fall and, striving always to be first, he will be in danger of running out of breath.

 Rooster/Rabbit

He will always keep his eyes peeled. He must always be entitled to the right to look, to control a situation and to feel he is the master of his destiny. He is not the kind to let himself be guided. He is a curious mixture in which the call of the dawn is coupled with the murmurs of the night. The voyage will be profitable if the prudence of the Rabbit is allied with the tenacity and loyalty of the Rooster. The Rabbit/Rooster is a generous, lively animal with a pure heart. His spur and his claw will be used defensively rather than offensively.

Rooster/Dragon

He only feels at ease in a high position, both in the geographic and the hierarchical sense of the term. He prefers the top of a tower or a top floor with terrace. The Rooster/Dragon will always be in the first row and nothing will escape his vigilant gaze; he will wish to dominate, control and supervise in all circumstances. He will be kind and possess originality, qualities which the Rooster does not always naturally cultivate. He will also be irresistibly charming.

 Rooster/Snake

An intuitive and frank animal, he will accomplish his tasks with a generous heart and with much good will and honesty — thus correcting the Snake's tendency to side-track — which will not prevent him from being uneasy, despite his apparent self-assurance. The Snake/Rooster flares up easily, so be careful if it is one of his bad days. He will attack with surprising aggressiveness and be entirely unjust simply to reassure himself. Do not attempt to expose his faults with evidence; he will be narrow-minded and never forgive you for having discovered his weak points. The Snake/Rooster is overly concerned with projecting a good image. He has a need to shine and surround himself with costly and beautiful things; this may appear superficial, but it is vital for his morale.

Rooster/Horse

While distinguished, loyal and generous, he is also vain and lacks modesty. His pride drives him, pushing him on against wind and tide, keeping him far in front of the masses, whom he needs to command and carry with him. The Horse/Rooster likes to stand out from the crowd; he is often unique and possesses a sense of honour to the highest degree; his word is his bond. His generosity can be total, his loyalty irreversible. If he gives you his confidence and friendship, nothing — no pressure nor catastrophe — will weaken it.

 Rooster/Goat

Generous and outgoing, this animal will be honest and pure, but, alas, his character will often prove unreliable and difficult to pin down. The Goat/Rooster will tend to kick out and back away, for he will not accept ties, advice or any form of dependency. His needs for liberty is expressed to a marked degree. He also needs to be reassured and coddled, but dislikes revealing his weaknesses and takes care not to expose himself. His principal motivation seems to be to set himself apart from other animals, for his pride will always win out. He wants to be original and fanciful at any price. If you are unlucky enough to come up against these qualities, he will become aggressive and capricious, even a bit cruel. However, he does not hold grudges and the next day you will see him trotting along, eyes shining and flowers for you in hand.

Rooster/Monkey

Very proud and full of himself, he will not be, to say the least, modest and self-effacing. He will see to it that he never goes unnoticed and will care a great deal about the effect he produces on others. Lacking neither intelligence nor good taste, he will still be irresistibly attracted by all that glitters. A word of advice: do not call too much attention to his weaknesses because the Monkey/Rooster will never forgive you!

 Rooster/Rooster

This animal will not pass unnoticed. Others will turn to look at the Rooster/Rooster, who is always dressed in the latest fashion, is rather proud, and tries to stand out among his companions — not because he scorns them, but simply because of his love for originality. He dreams constantly of always being in the forefront, in a high position, at the top of a tree or tower. He is a symbol of vigilance, both protector and look-out. But he will often be aggressive, susceptible, intolerant and rebellious if contradicted. Alert to the external world, he may close up within himself due to his fear of discovering his own weaknesses, as well as those of others.

Rooster/Dog

Imbued with honour and fidelity, the Dog/Rooster will be a sentinel and guardian, yet capable of questioning his handsome self-assurance and looking into himself and tempering his aggressiveness. He will make his way by night as well as day, straddling the two worlds of shade and sun. He will be belligerent, pessimistic and active, but the ordeals he endures will not discourage him. He will persevere, but without any wish for conquest or revenge. The Dog/Rooster will seek to improve himself but remain susceptible to those around him. He will be a man of his word and of his heart.

 Rooster/Pig

He is a strange and solitary traveller, due more to personal conviction than to a love of originality. The Rooster/Pig seeks to stand out in a crowd by his attitude towards life rather than by appearance. In order to achieve this, he will seek a hiding place in which to bury his treasures, far from the eyes of the world. He will work hard to acquire wealth and knowledge, but will take care to disguise them so as to be the only one to enjoy them — an expression of his pride and egotism.

THE ROOSTER
AND THE FIVE
ELEMENTS

五行

YOUR ELEMENT

In Chinese astrology, each year is joined to an Element. There are five Elements: *Water, Fire, Wood, Metal, Earth.*

Each of the twelve emblematic animals is linked successively to each of the five Elements. For example, in the year 1900 the Rat was Earth, in 1912 he was Fire; in 1924 he was Metal, in 1936, Water and in 1948 he was Wood. Therefore, for the twelve years from 1900 he was linked to Earth, for the next twelve years to Fire, and, for every succeeding period of twelve years, to each of the other Elements, in succession.

In order to determine the Element corresponding to the year of your birth, use the table below:

> *Years whose digits end in:* 1 and 6 — Water
>
> 2 and 7 — Fire
>
> 3 and 8 — Wood
>
> 4 and 9 — Metal
>
> 5 and 0 — Earth

The same union of *Animal-Element* repeats every sixty years, for example, Rat-Earth appeared in 1720, 1780, 1840, 1900, 1960 and so on.

The five Elements are the primary forces affecting the universe. It is their particular association with each of the signs which provides the basis for every horoscope. Movement and fluctuation, Yin and Yang, these symbolic forces are in a perpetual state of action and interaction.

Wood gives birth to Fire, which gives birth to Earth, which gives birth to Metal, which gives birth to Water, which in turn gives birth to Wood.

ROOSTER/WATER
(you were born in 1921 or 1981)

The cold born of the northern sky descended to earth and gave birth to Water. The Chinese consider Water more a synonym for coldness and ice than a symbol of fertility.

Characteristics of the Rooster/Water

Water of winter nights, rigour and severity, calm and deep Water to be feared and respected, still Water sheltering underwater demons asleep in its depths, foetid and muddy Water of the marshes, a refuge of crawling creatures. The Rooster/Water, of the Yang tendency, will not risk being immobilized by his Element; rather, he will seek to make use of its dynamic aspect. For him, Water will be fresh and sparkling, a symbol of movement and youth. After all, Water is needed to make the grain grow, which in turn feeds the Rooster.

Health of the Rooster/Water

The Water organ is the kidney; its flavour is salty. The Rooster should remain dynamic and active. Water must circulate through him; he must take care to avoid blockages and be careful of what he eats.

The Rooster/Water and others

The Rooster/Water should take himself in hand and moderate his aggressiveness and avoid excesses; he should learn to manage his life calmly and serenely. It will be possible for the Rooster to govern the masses (which he dreams of doing), if he places his pride and honour in the service of men and justice and seeks to improve social conditions and human relations. The Rooster/Water will be a humanist rather than a mystic. He will prefer the concrete, excel in manual work and remain honest throughout his career. The Rooster/Water is not a man of compromises and does not mind becoming personally involved and taking responsibility for his actions. Thus he is first and foremost a man who acts from the heart.

Advice for a Rooster/Water

Like your Element, Water, you are pure and possess the energy necessary to direct, command and control. Do not ruin these gifts because of your pride.

A Rooster/Water year

The culminating point for a Rooster/Water year will be winter, a period of gestation. The Yin of Water will balance the Yang of the Rooster.

Turn towards what is dynamic and do not allow yourself to be attracted by sleeping waters, which are too still for your needs. Take the time to reflect upon yourself and your life. Relax by gardening, for example.

Historical example of a Rooster/Water year 1981

The English Labour party, fractured within and open to every form of dissension under a leader so obtuse that he regarded it his duty to stay where he was, awaited the results of the French presidential election. The Americans had moved decisively to the right when they voted for Reagan and the English no less so when deciding for Margaret Thatcher. If President Giscard d'Estaing was returned to office the Labour left in England could claim to be the true voice crying in the wilderness of Western reaction. However, if Mitterand succeeded, his old-fashioned policies would surely founder as had those of previous Labour governments in England, cast in the same model; and all the more so since Mitterand would have time to implement them, the guaranteed continuity of power given by de Gaulle's constitution. Thus the prospect of a Socialist victory in France did not really appeal to the English Socialists. The moderates preferred that their own failed policies should not be given, as it were, a re-run in France; the extremists sought the martyr's garb which a strong Socialist government in France would render otiose.

The French Communists formed an extension to these equations. The stronger they proved to be in a government formed by Mitterand the more they could be blamed for the failure of its policies, a result therefore satisfactory to the moderates in the Labour party; whereas the weaker their representation, the more persecuted they would appear, a result which would suit the English Left. Such were the political equations being composed in England in 1981.

The significance of Mitterand's victory for Anglo-French relations lay in the possibility of a new approach, freed from the long shadows of the Gaullist past. It certainly led to an increase in candour during the early exchanges between the President and the English Prime Minister.

ROOSTER/WOOD
(you were born in 1933)

To the East, the wind blew in the sky and from its warm caress of the the earth Wood was born.

Characteristics of the Rooster/Wood

Wood is of the morning and of springtime. Its temperate nature loves harmony and beauty. This Element is flattering for the preening Rooster, so careful of his appearance. This season will be fruitful and creative if the Rooster blends with and becomes impregnated by the beauty surrounding him, opening himself to an internal world whose door he tends to leave closed. However, Wood is also passionate, susceptible and excessive, and the Rooster already possesses these defects. He should use his clear-sightedness to avoid letting himself get carried away. But the Rooster/Wood knows his limits, which will doubtlessly permit him to maintain his equilibrium, giving him self-assurance and an ability to share with and love others.

Health of the Rooster/Wood
The organ of Wood is the liver; its flavour is acid. An awareness of your weaknesses should not cause you to become anxious or depressed and indulge in over-eating.

The Rooster/Wood and others
The Rooster/Wood will often behave calmly and seem sure of himself. But this is misleading, for at certain moments he is full of self-doubts. His self-assured attitude, which is purely defensive, will be pleasing for those around him, who will enjoy his relaxed and smiling air. He will have a talent for improvising in difficult situations. He has a fine imagination, which he will put to use, particularly if he turns towards the arts, such as poetry or painting. He will take refuge in nature in order to fulfil his need for liberty, space and harmony.

Some advice for a Rooster/Wood
Your unaffected nature increases your charm; maintain your simplicity and live at your own rhythm. Refuse to put on an iron collar or a coat of armour — you are not made for them.

A Rooster/Wood year
The culminating point for a Rooster/Wood year is spring, a period of growth and prosperity.

Profit from this year to recharge your batteries. Be creative, discover Mother Nature and do not give in to anger; be supple, tolerant and seek harmony.

Historical example of a Rooster/Wood year 1453

In Constantinople the roses were in bloom as the month of May drew to a close but the moon, once the symbol of the thousand year old city, was on the wane. After seven weeks of siege by the Turkish armies, led by the young Sultan Mehmet, the hopes of the Christians within the walls were fading. Yet there was a feeling of frustration in the Turkish camp. Badly damaged though they were by the great siege engines set against them, the city walls had not yet been penetrated by a single Turkish soldier. It was known that the old Vizier Halil continued to disapprove of the venture; relief might be on the way; a Venetian fleet was reported at Chios; the Hungarians might cross the Danube.

Mehmet attempted a last overture for peace which neither he nor the Emperor believed in. He then met with his commanders and notables. Zaganos Pasha and the younger generals called for an immediate assault, and Mehmet acceded to their views. His heralds toured the army and, as the customs of Islam allowed, promised a three-day sack of the city. Monday was declared a day of rest and atonement and the troops were ordered to be ready for the assault the following day. Mehmet again spoke to his ministers and commanders. He reminded them of the booty which would soon be theirs, that the city was not impregnable, that its defenders were few and exhausted, and that for centuries its capture had been the sacred duty of the faithful. He personally would never give up the fight until the city was taken.

On Monday, while quietness pervaded the Moslem camp, a great procession was formed in Constantinople and the icons and sacred objects carried through the streets. The Emperor likewise spoke to his people and to his Greek and Italian commanders, of their duty to die for their faith, their families, their country and their sovereign. The populace moved to a service of intercession held in the great church of the Holy Wisdom, heedless that its sacred liturgy had been defiled by the Latins. For this moment before destruction there was unity in the Church of Constantinople.

The afternoon of the following day Mehmet entered the city, heir and possessor of the ancient Roman Empire.

ROOSTER/FIRE
(you were born in 1957)

Heat was born in the southern sky, descended to earth and fertilized it. From their union, Fire was born.

Characteristics of the Rooster/Fire

The Fire Element is of the midday, of the South, of summer. Fire is Yang; it is the Element that warms, burns, animates, quickens, transforms and overthrows. Fire in a Rooster of the Yang tendency will strengthen his rashness, audacity and argumentativeness. This could be dangerous, because the Fire might devour, becoming a violent and flashing power. The Rooster/Fire should learn to control this force which can flare up within him and could turn against him. If he allows it to gain the upper hand it could be transformed into aggressiveness and be destructive to others as well as to himself.

Health of the Rooster/Fire

The organ of Fire is the heart, its flavour is bitter. Fire of summer and of the South, Yang plus Yang; be careful of over-work and excesses of all kinds. If you burn your wings, you may well lose your feathers.

The Rooster/Fire and others

He will often be violent and passionate. His life will not be easy: although he needs to be surrounded by flattery and applause, he is also aware of his weaknesses and thus the admiration of others ends by making him scornful and sceptical. The Fire Element will strengthen the belligerence of the Rooster/Fire: he can be a man of action, a soldier or a formidable leader; but the Rooster/Fire can also be an outsider who likes to stand apart as a means of seducing and conquering. He will often be an exceptional person, an adventurer of wide-open spaces or of the intellect. Gifted with a strange and powerful personality, he will evolve within a special universe, far from other men and their run-of-the-mill reactions.

Advice for a Rooster/Fire

Warrior, statesman, emperor or revolutionary, you run after phantoms that you can never grasp. This is the basis for your greatest successes as well as for your worst failures. Be especially vigilant and discerning.

A Rooster/Fire year

The culminating point for a Rooster/Fire year will be summer, a period of creation.

This will be an active and enriching year, both materially and spiritually, and you will be full of energy. However, do not do too much nor spread yourself too thin or you will tire and lose confidence.

Historical example of a Rooster/Fire year 1477

This was a period, both in England and France, of rapidly shifting alliances. Actions at least nominally traitorous were prompted by a political climate so uncertain that the principle of loyalty had little, if any, relevance. By 1474 Edward IV had secured his position in England. By good luck and good generalship he had weathered the Lancastrian revolutions — their king was dead, his supporters scattered and the power of the Neville family destroyed for ever.

The embers of the old war between England and France remained, potent if dulled. Edward's policy was to revive the war once he had secured his position at home. The rivalry between Louis XI of France and Charles the Bold of Burgundy offered him his opportunity. He and Charles made a firm agreement to invade the territories of the French king in 1475. The money was raised, a large army collected together and Edward crossed to Calais. But, as

Louis recognized, Edward's resources were already stretched. If Edward could be detached by a bribe he would be free to deal with his main enemy who would then be isolated. In consideration of a large payment and a pension Edward withdrew his army.

Thus it was that Charles of Burgundy, already committed to an act of insurrection, found that this principal ally had deserted him. In his chagrin he set about antagonizing the very people who might still have rallied to him. In 1477 he arrived before Nantes with a depleted force, as weary as his treasury was impoverished. Duc René of Lorraine lay in wait for him, supported by German and Swiss contingents. Charles was slain and his army melted away. Louis had won his victory; money had detached Edward and money had secured the services of the German and Swiss mercenaries.

ROOSTER/EARTH
(you were born in 1945)

Earth was born from the slowly falling Elements of the sky at its humid zenith.

Characteristics of the Rooster/Earth
This is an afternoon Earth, the humid and hot Earth of summer. It is the symbol of the well-cushioned, soft nest, of comfort and abundance; an Earth of slow and profound transformations.

The Rooster/Earth will not be much of an adventurer: he will be afraid of becoming too involved and of taking risks. He often will be rather egotistical. Mainly preoccupied with his own success, security and appearance, he will not hesitate to profit from others' work, and will not be overly imaginative. However, the Rooster's vivacity will encourage the flourishing of his body, mind and heart. He will have a tendency to bury his treasures and wealth away from indiscreet glances: his Element will be less a symbol of meditation and reflection than a safe deposit box or Ali Baba's cave.

Health of the Rooster/Earth
The Earth's organ is the spleen, its flavour is sweet. The Rooster/Earth should not remain immobile or he may suffer from sluggishness and become fat in his old age.

The Rooster/Earth and others
He will be realistic, pragmatic, and often shrewd rather than intelligent. Due to his egotism, he will not be burdened with too many principles. Moreover, he will be prudent and distrustful; he will reflect at length, carefully weighing the pro's and con's before becoming involved in any enterprise. He will rapidly climb to the top in professions such as banking, property or insurance, not hesitating to elbow others out of the way. If a Rooster/Earth goes into politics he will be successful, especially in the economic sector. He seems to be loyal and sincere; he needs an activity which flatters his pride while assuring him fame and comfort. As a parent, the Rooster/Earth will be rather authoritarian, sometimes smothering his children with care.

Advice for a Rooster/Earth
Fulfil your heart's desire and become a man in the public eye. By expressing your need to be seen and admired, perhaps you will succeed in unlocking certain internal tensions and exorcizing your terrible fear of poverty. Otherwise, become a rich farmer.

A Rooster/Earth year
The culminating point for a Rooster/Earth year will be summer.

It will be a favourable time for the Rooster, who will no longer need to worry about how he is to eat. Freed from this constraint, the Rooster/Earth should overcome his egotism, open his heart and enlarge his horizons beyond his 'territory'.

Historical example of a Rooster/Earth year 1945

At the Potsdam conference in July the decision was taken to drop the first two atomic bombs on Japanese cities. Hiroshima was annihilated on 5 August; 'sweet Nagasaki, the flower of Kuyushu' four days later. The barbarism extended by Hitler and the SS to Europe was now extended by the Americans and their international team of scientists to Japan.

In August 1945 Japan was, for all practical purposes defeated and ready to sue for terms — but 'terms' there could not be because the doctrine of unconditional surrender enforced on Germany had also to be enforced on Japan. In that context, Churchill's reaction when hearing of the successful testing of the bomb at Los Alamos is understandable: he recorded that 'the nightmare vision of conventional air bombing and invasion by huge armies had vanished.' More important to the Americans, Japan could be defeated without the help of the Russians. It was altogether clear that the Americans, whatever they would agree to in Europe, had no wish for a Russian presence in Japan. To these considerations the scientists added their own: 'The bomb simply had to be a success — so much money had been expended on it . . . the relief to everyone concerned when the bomb was finished and dropped was enormous.'* That was the view of one engaged on the project. Truman's chief of staff Admiral Leary emphasized that the military were anxious to demonstrate the bomb's effectiveness — two billion dollars had been spent on it.

Dropped, demonstrated or kept in store, there is no doubt that the technology of the bomb could not have been kept a secret. Stalin knew of its development and his agents were deployed to gather the information needed. The balance of terror would have dominated postwar strategy whether or not the bomb had been used. Yet its actual release was a gesture of moral impotence from which the victors have never recovered.

* B. Liddell Hart in *New Cambridge Modern History*, vol.XII, 1968.

ROOSTER/METAL
(you were born in 1909 or 1969)

In the sky, coming from the West, drought grazed the skin of the earth and gave birth to Metal. Winds come from the faraway steppes seeking the vital sap.

Characteristics of the Rooster/Metal

Metal is of the night, of autumn and of cold. It symbolizes clarity, purity and precision. The Rooster/Metal will fluctuate between beauty and destruction, with an appetite for material success and a need for spiritual fulfilment. He will suffer because he is a realist and painfully clear-sighted. The Metal Element tends to encase him in an iron collar, to cut him off from his roots and to push him into a desperate quest for the sap of vitality, for contact with the earth, which resembles an obsession for a lost paradise. The Rooster/Metal may therefore find himself bound within a psychological prison made up of constraints and rigidity. These qualities, however, are not in the Rooster's nature, being as he is attracted to society, sophistication and luxury. He will therefore feel torn, lost and ill-at-ease. In order to recuperate and bandage his wounds he will be forced to endure periods of solitude or retreat to create the harmony to which his body and soul aspire.

Health of the Rooster/Metal

The organ of Metal is the lung, its flavour is pungent. The Rooster/Metal should pay attention to his heart and his breathing because he seeks an equilibrium which is difficult to attain.

The Rooster/Metal and others

The Rooster/Metal is energetic, a man of his word and an honest and sincere friend. But he is not very sensitive to the simple beauty of things; he must always have structures, a fixed framework, regulations and reasons. Not much of a diplomat, he will make decisions, without taking special cases or attenuating circumstances into account. He will like to command, programme and organize everything. He will leave little space in his life for chance; in fact, he insists that everything depend upon *his* decisions. He often lacks an awareness of subtleties and depends mostly on his critical faculties. In short, he will not be agreeable to live with because he is as demanding of those close to him as he is of himself.

A Rooster/Metal year

The culminating point for a Rooster/Metal year will be autumn.

Do not neglect your physical form; do the necessary exercises, for this will improve your general equilibrium. Take care not to be too excessive or you will stiffen and suffer from an erroneous vision of the world. Take time to listen to your body and your heart. In this way you will become more sensitive to the needs of others.

Historical example of a Rooster/Metal year 1789

On 5 May, after many delays, the Estates General of France assembled at Versailles. The event was taken note of but not particularly remarked on in the capitals of Europe. Little more than two months later the Bastille was stormed and the most stratified society in western Europe extinguished. Mirabeau's pledge to 'yield only to the bayonet' had been fulfilled. In August the National Assembly formally abolished the feudal orders of France and relieved the peasantry of its ancient obligations to the seigneurial system. Thenceforth, all classes in France were free from restrictions in terms of office holding and trade. The events of 14 July were thus ratified. The public administration ceased to function, the army declared itself dissolved and the National Guard, created by Lafayette to temper the wilder enthusiasms of the Revolution, comprehensively embodied those who were the most prone to them.

The French Revolution was the first in the modern world to demonstrate the power of radicalism — not to reform by degrees but to overthrow by violence.

The English radicals responded with enthusiasm; a vigorous correspondence developed with members of the new regime. The French even followed English example and established political clubs. But English enthusiasm responded to the spirit rather than the substance of the revolution. By temperament the English radicals were attached to the constitution embodied in the 'Glorious Revolution' of 1688; they were proud to be its heirs and were not alone in thinking that the French would be content to accept it as a model. The Americans had a better understanding of events and good cause for pride when the French declaration of the Rights of Man was published on 2 August. It closely followed the Virginia Bill of Rights of 1776.

Analogical Table
of the Different Elements

Elements	Wood	Fire	Earth	Metal	Water
Years ending in	3 and 8	2 and 7	0 and 5	4 and 9	1 and 6
Colours	Green	Red	Yellow	White	Blue
Seasons	Spring	Summer	End of summer	Autumn	Winter
Climates	Wind	Heat	Humid	Dry	Cold
Flavours	Acid	Bitter	Sweet	Pungent	Salty
Principal organ	Liver	Heart	Spleen	Lungs	Kidneys
Secondary organ	Gallbladder	Small intestine	Stomach	Large intestine	Bladder
Food	Wheat, poultry	Rice, lamb	Corn, beef	Oats, horse	Peas, pork

Table of Harmony Between the Elements

	Wood Female	Fire Female	Earth Female	Metal Female	Water Female
Male Wood	●●	○	○○○	○	○○
Male Fire	○	○	○○	●	●●
Male Earth	●●	○○	○	○○○	●
Male Metal	○	●●	●	●●	○○○
Male Water	○	●●	●	○○○	○

Legend:

- ○○○ Excellent prosperity
- ○○ Good harmony, understanding
- ○ Effort needed
- ● Rivalries and problems of reciprocal domination
- ●● Misunderstanding and incomprehension

THE
FOUR SEASONS
OF
THE ROOSTER

四季

If you were born in spring

Rooster/Aries

This alliance considerably magnifies the qualities and defects of the Rooster, for he has many points in common with Aries.

The Rooster/Aries is above all courageous: he will face up to the most desperate situations, behaving heroically and with an awareness of the useless but nevertheless superb gesture. In this he resembles the hero of a cloak-and-dagger film. He is sincere and never lies; when in love he will never express feelings that he does not have. But he is often disappointed in love, for, being idealistic and naive, he is easy to fool; moreover, he cannot understand why anyone would lie or disguise their feelings. And here we begin to perceive his defects.

The Rooster/Aries is so exasperatingly frank that he can become a danger to himself and to others. He is also totally unaware of the sensitivity and vulnerability of others. It is difficult not to become enraged when he starts to tell you a few home truths; but he should be forgiven because he does not hurt you on purpose.

Rooster/Taurus

This is a stable and warm Rooster, an epicurean who likes the good things in life. He derives great satisfaction from helping people and will never refuse assistance. If you are in a horrible situation he will stand by your side, cheer you up and hold your hand. But if things are going well for you, he will not accept any capricious behaviour. The Rooster/Taurus is courageous and energetic; he also does not like to waste precious time and is therefore permeated with the idea of utility. Like all Roosters he has the unfortunate habit of hitting his friends over their heads with rather indigestible truths, which are usually based on long observation and almost always true. Yet he does not wish to hurt anyone's feelings, and if he realizes that he has, while he will not excuse himself, he will do something especially nice in order to be forgiven.

The Rooster/Taurus loves his liberty but needs to feel admired and appreciated. He is secretly hypersensitive. Extremely sensual and sociable, he loves to receive friends and is a fine host. He would also like to have a harem, to which he would be marvellously faithful.

Rooster/Gemini

This Rooster is a bit of a weather-vane, not because he is constantly changing his opinions, but because he is always moving. He is hyperactive and so full of contradictory plans that he seems agitated, and therefore can become tiring. Living with him is like sharing a house with a pneumatic drill.

The Rooster/Gemini is always prepared to do something, whether it be brilliant or stupid. However, do not misunderstand him: he is agitated, but also fairly constant in his affections. As long as he is allowed to spin around as he pleases he remains attached to his hens and is not interested in those belonging to his neighbours. He is enthusiastic, but also a dreamer; dreaming about everything fascinating that he might do — and he usually ends up doing it, for at bottom he has good common sense. Despite his detached air he is rather clever in business — he has a good 'nose' for it.

Extremely obliging, he is easy to live with because he leaves others in peace. He asks only one thing — that you do the same for him. His kindness is based on a solid foundation of egotism: 'Charity begins at home'.

If you were born in summer
Rooster/Cancer

In order to achieve material and emotional success, the Rooster/Cancer must first overcome his contradictions, which is not easy. He is, in fact, particularly sensitive, vulnerable and vindictive. Disappointments often have an indelible effect on him, and for this reason he needs to be praised and reassured. However, this is difficult because he is so emotional and subjective that he cannot adapt easily to new circumstances or surroundings. A homebody, and basically a conformist, he is the kind who never leaves the barnyard, while dreaming of being a bird of paradise, flying over exotic lands.

The Rooster/Cancer has tenacity and inner strength, but needs time to think about what he is going to do, which can make him seem passive or absent-minded. Take care! If you attack his family he will become a fighting cock. He is never so happy as when surrounded by members of his family. As long as he is treated with respect and kindness he is affectionate, tender and stable. Tell him that you love him and smooth his feathers; this adorable person lacks self-confidence and may wear himself out showing off if he feels unappreciated.

Rooster/Leo

All Roosters are slightly vain and appreciate luxury. Leos are also proud — and love luxury. In other words, if he is born in a slum, the Rooster/Leo will not rest until he has escaped from it. His dream is to live in a penthouse atop a pure gold building, where he can crow out loud to show off his success. This may seem like a defect, but it is often a form of wisdom — knowing how to be satisfied with what one has accomplished.

The Rooster/Leo is honest and even possesses a certain nobility. He is always aware of the effect he is going to produce, and he wants that effect to be good. Of course he is an egotist, like all Roosters, but in his case it is less obvious because he wishes to appear generous and magnanimous. He succeeds in this, and it is only those who are extremely close to him who understand that giving pleasure to others reassures him and gives him a good opinion of himself.

At work, the Rooster/Leo is authoritarian and energetic. He has only concrete dreams; his building is solid and you can live safely within it.

Rooster/Virgo

A Virgo born in a year of the Rooster will gain self-confidence and the dash of audacity that he usually lacks in order to succeed. But his confidence is only a facade, for the Rooster/Virgo is an anxious individual. He works and works, never stopping for an instant, imposing strict discipline on himself and his subordinates. This is because he does not know what tomorrow may bring.

He might be thought modest, but this is not really true for Virgo is a summer sign and it is those Roosters born in the spring who are less flamboyant. In fact, the Rooster/Virgo needs to shine, but only among a select few. He crows quietly, but he does crow; try to silence him and you will see — he will attack you immediately. The Rooster/Virgo is madly attached to his principles and ideas and will not accept being contradicted. Be a good friend and leave him his crutches, which are so well waxed.

If you were born in autumn
Rooster/Libra

At first glance this alliance seems extremely positive. Those born under the sign of Libra are diplomatic and have a sharp awareness of subtleties. It is rare to find a Libra taking an extreme position, which will be favourable for the Rooster who so often overstates his case. This does not mean, however, that a Rooster/Libra is a tactful and delicate spokesman, but at least he will try to avoid exaggerating and will not shock too many people.

The Rooster/Libra is extremely talkative; he loves to discuss and argue, but he does not say just anything. He could be a good lawyer or orator. He is sometimes slightly ostentatious and is very concerned with his appearance and his home; he is rather spendthrift where his comfort is concerned. Rather prudent for a Rooster, he will nevertheless behave somewhat stupidly when in love because of his tendency to judge others by their appearance and to idealize them.

The Rooster/Libra is very much a conformist and he always remains well within the law. In fact, he would be happy as a lark if he were given a medal or decoration.

Rooster/Scorpio

A piece of advice: before starting a discussion with a Rooster/Scorpio, watch where you are walking; and while you are at it, avoid competing with him. He is formidable: first, because he is energetic and courageous; second, because he knows how to wield authority and make others behave as he wishes. Above all he is a smooth talker and his gift of the gab is incredible! His critical faculties are easily provoked, and his latent aggressiveness is expressed in his speech. He can appear to be extremely disagreeable. This is not always the case, but he does take a lot of pleasure in cutting people to the quick, even when they are relatives or friends. The only remedy is to burst out laughing and reply sharply with a smile. He will not mind, for he has a sense of humour — black, naturally.

The Rooster/Scorpio likes to dominate and to this end tries to surprise people and catch them up short when they least expect it. Consequently he is often misunderstood because at bottom he is insecure, above all when in love. If he is master of the barnyard, his hens will be plump and contented; but if he is running wild, he will wreak havoc in all the neighbouring hen-houses. This is an important thing to know about him.

Rooster/Sagittarius

He is the most boastful of the Roosters. He never stops talking about his projects, which, of course, are grandiose. He may plan to convert the entire world, to fight for humanity's survival, but even this is too modest for him; words such as 'cosmos', 'universe', and so on are more like it. At a party he will tell you in a whisper — loudly enough so that others will overhear — about his last meeting with some extra-terrestrials. He is not a liar, simply enthusiastic — and slightly excitable.

However, the Rooster/Sagittarius rarely carries out his mad plans, for he likes his comfort. He is an adventurer only in a dream world of his own making; he is unequalled when it comes to telling stories to children.

This warm-hearted, relaxed, independent person has a lot of charm, but he needs liberty, especially during his adolescence. As he matures he can become slightly dogmatic and want to make everyone else profit from the fruits of his experience. But he is always ready to take care of orphans in distress. His courage, loyalty and fidelity to his friends make it easy to excuse his blunders.

If you were born in winter
Rooster/Capricorn
The Rooster's tendency to boast too much in this case is transformed into a sort of iciness. The Rooster/Capricorn is just and full of integrity, but he cares little for subtleties. His outrageous frankness if not appreciated by most people, especially since it tends to be irreproachable. He is not really hard and actually has a good heart and is a faithful and dependable friend. But his innate honesty makes it impossible for him to tell white lies or to twist the truth.

He is also the most hard-working and clear-sighted of all the Roosters. Obsessed with the desire to finish what he has started, he cannot stop working. He is a perfectioniist who is as interested in the means as the end result.

The Rooster/Capricorn is well-liked socially, for he is courteous and behaves with ease and discretion; also, his conversation is interesting because he always knows what he is talking about. Some Rooster/Capricorns have a tendency to philosophize and to play with abstract ideas; their intellectual life may then be richer than their emotional life which is sown with periods of solitude.

Rooster/Aquarius
The alliance of these two signs considerably increases the tendency in both to be idealistic. The Rooster/Aquarius is an

absolute idealist who thinks sincerely and generously of the well-being of humanity in general, and of his friends and relations in particular. Although he does not launch into mad adventures like the Rooster/Sagittarius, he is willing to give a great deal of himself in order to arrange things for others. His mind is full of ingenious ideas destined to lessen the hardships of life, both on a practical and human level. He is a born advisor, filled with amiable intentions, good-will and devotion — all of it crowned with a good dose of naiveté. He has an answer for everything and adores being asked for his opinion or advice, but he sometimes lacks logic and objectivity.

Socially, the Rooster/Aquarius is amiable and eloquent; he gives the impression of knowing a great many things; he is as good at listening as he is at talking, which is always agreeable for others.

On the other hand, this master of conversation is not very reliable on an emotional level. Because he likes to give pleasure, he has a tendency to promise more than he can give, and will then disappear like smoke as soon as his back is up against the wall.

Rooster/Pisces

This is an elusive Rooster who is difficult to catch. His feathers are smooth, damp scales and impossible to grasp. However, he has great qualities: he is humane, sensitive and devoted. He will listen to you compassionately for hours as you recount your miseries, and will then give you his opinion, sprinkling it with reflections in the style of 'of course, I am not sure', 'perhaps I am mistaken', and the like. And that precisely is his problem: he is unsure of himself. He is often torn between two choices, one romantic, the other materialistic. He never really knows whether he is a bird of prey or a victim, whether he is going to sacrifice himself or cheerfully eat everyone up.

He is a dreamer and a scatter-brain, sometimes here, sometimes there. Those around him sometimes have an intense desire to tie him to his perch. But even then he would escape — in his thoughts.

The Rooster/Pisces is very talkative. He lets go a river of words which flow and seduce, for he likes to please and is a master at it. Never caught off guard, clearheaded and resourceful beneath his dreamy exterior, he will always survive — but not without scars.

THE
I CHING

易经

THE I CHING AND THE ROOSTER

In the I Ching game, you ask a question and you obtain an answer. It is therefore a divining game. But the question you ask is posed through your Rooster identity; the wheels, the complex mechanism of your mind and spirit, begin to turn. You ask a Rooster question and the I Ching answers with a Rooster 'solution', on which you then meditate as a Rooster before arriving at a Rooster conclusion.

The player is presented with a hexagram which contains the 'hypothesis-response' to his question, or, more exactly, a synthesis of forces affecting the concern or event inquired about.

For you, Master Rooster, here are the sixty-four hexagrams of the I Ching and sixty-four Rooster hypotheses.

How to proceed
1. The question
Ask a question regarding any problem at all, past, present or future, personally concerning you. (If the question concerns a friend, consult the I Ching game in the book corresponding to his Chinese sign.)

2. Method of play
It must be done with concentration.
Take **three ordinary and similar coins** — for example, three 50p coins.
Heads will equal the number 3.
Tails will equal the number 2.
Throw the coins.
If the result is two coins showing Heads and one Tails, write 3 + 3 + 2. You thus obtain a total of 8 which you represent by a continuous line: ——— .
Draw the same continuous line if you have three coins showing Heads (3 + 3 + 3 = 9).

If you throw two coins showing Tails and one Heads
$(2+2+3=7)$, or all three showing Tails $(2+2+2=6)$, draw
two separate lines: ▬ ▬ .

To sum up, 8 and 9 correspond to: ▬▬▬▬ (Yin)

6 and 7 correspond to: ▬ ▬ (Yang)

Repeat this operation *six times*, noting at the time of each
throw the figure obtained on a piece of paper, proceeding
from the first to the sixth figure, from bottom to top.

The final result, including a trigram from the bottom, or

lower trigram (example: ▬▬▬), and a trigram of the top,

or upper trigram (example: ▬▬▬), will be a hexagram of
the I Ching. In our example this would look like:

Now merely look for the hexagram number in the table on
page 78 , and then consult the list of hexagrams with their
descriptions to find the given answer. *In our example,* the
hexagram obtained is number 63, entitled **After completion**.

Table of Hexagrams

Trigrams	Upper lines ☰	☷	☳
Lower lines			
☰	1	11	34
☷	12	2	16
☳	25	24	51
☵	6	7	40
☶	33	15	62
☴	44	46	32
☲	13	36	55
☱	10	19	54

Use this table to find the number of your hexagrams. The meeting point between the lower and upper trigrams indicates the number of the hexagram that you are seeking.

☵	☶	☴	☲	☱
5	26	9	14	43
8	23	20	35	45
3	27	42	21	17
29	4	59	64	47
39	52	53	56	31
48	18	57	50	28
63	22	37	30	49
60	41	61	38	58

THE HEXAGRAMS OF THE ROOSTER

CH'IEN

1 *The creative:* Energy, strength and will. You are the symbol of K, signifying the five virtues — so do not impatiently claw the air with your spurs.

K'UN

2 *The receptive:* You who sing to welcome the sunrise cannot be unaware that the heat of the sun regenerates the Mother Earth which bears us.

CHUN

3 *Initial difficulty:* Master Rooster will know how to disentangle himself from the straw — on condition that he looks closely at himself and recognizes his errors.

MÊNG

4 *Youthful folly:* 'It is not I who seeks the young fool, but the young fool who seeks me.' Although you are master of the hen-house, do not rise on tiptoe and puff out your feathers — bravado will not dissolve the danger.

HSÜ

5 *Waiting:* What you expect will come by day, but it would be ridiculous to sing too soon. You would be laughed at, and your pride would not stand for that.

SUNG

6 *Conflict:* Although combat is your domain, do not make a principle of it; there are wiser and gentler methods.

SHIH

7 *The army:* You are the emblem, the flag. Submission and discipline should not be a problem for you — and leaders are always needed.

PI

8 *Holding together (union):* This is a word you know well. The moment is ripe to assemble all your available forces and to seek out your friends.

SHIAO CH'U

9 *The taming power of the small:* Widen your horizons; do not say that the earth is too small while you remain on your perch.

LÜ

10 *Treading:* 'Tread on the tail of the Tiger, he does not bite man.' If you wish to obtain someone's support, do not stiffen your crest nor puff out your feathers; pull in your spurs and do not utter ear-piercing cries.

T'AI

11 *Peace:* Dig your trenches, build your barricades; do not hesitate to surround yourself with protective barriers.

P'I

12 *Standstill:* If it is difficult to stand on a promontory, climb down and wait comfortably until the storm has passed. Otherwise, nothing can break your fall.

THE ROOSTER

T'UNG JÊN

13 *Fellowship with men:* 'Community with men in broad daylight brings success.' Any sincere alliance will be profitable to you.

TA YU

14 *Possession in great measure:* If you inherit a 'full granary' do not be in a hurry to empty it to celebrate a windfall; instead, make it bear fruit.

CH'IEN

15 *Modesty:* Seek to completely relax any physical, emotional or mental tensions. This is difficult to achieve when perched on high. Find a happy medium, but do not use this to show off your feathers.

YÜ

16 *Enthusiasm:* The Rooster is exhilarated, and he knows how to make others share in his excitement. But more is expected: some initiative, ideas and responsibility.

SUI

17 *Following:* Your powers of seduction and your fine presence will get the better of others' reticence. When you really want to, you know how to play with words without hurting anyone's feelings.

KU

18 *Work on what has been spoiled:* Do not accuse your friends of having been asleep and allowing the fox into the hen-house while you continue to take sleeping pills.

LIN

19 *The approach:* The sun may shine in the midst of clouds, but it will not prevent rain from falling. This is the moment to sharpen your discrimination.

KUAN

20 *Contemplation:* Perch on the top of the tower; you will enjoy a wider view. But do not show yourself on the day of the hunt.

SHIH HO

21 *Biting through (or clearly defined penalties):* Stand up; fight with your spurs and your beak; set an example. Your sense of honour cannot endure lying, and your righteousness is horrified by false promises.

PI

22 *Grace:* You are sensitive to appearances and all that glitters. Scratch through the varnish, scour the facade, strip and analyse. Truth is so much more beautiful when naked.

PO

23 *Splitting apart:* Do not undertake anything; the terrain is unhealthy and the edifice fragile; even the grain is mouldy and the water foetid.

FU

24 *Return — the turning point:* The shower has stopped. Profit from the return of the sun: the elements are once again lucky for you. Learn how to pardon and recognize your errors.

THE ROOSTER

WU WANG

25 *Innocence:* Even if one is intuitive one does not necessarily possess the truth. Do not try to impose your opinions on your neighbours.

TA CH'U

26 *The taming power of the great:* Power and strength. You are honest and a man of your word; you are going to be able to prove it, but you must avoid rigidity and introversion. What is good for you is not necessarily good for those around you.

I

27 *The corners of the mouth:* Food for the body and the mind. You are neither a camel, a boa constrictor, nor a walking encylcopaedia. The moral is: absorb what you need; an insatiable appetite will give you apoplexy.

TA KUO

28 *Preponderance of the great:* You are the symbol of the warrior, but this is no reason to attack your own terrain by boasting. Do not do more than what is asked of you.

K'AN

29 *The fathomless water:* Be vigilant and on guard; there is aggression in the air. But do not change your itinerary: you know your route, but you ignore the dangers outside of it.

LI

30 *The clinging, fire:* Do not exhaust yourself by beating your wings and emitting ferocious war cries; perhaps the attack was a sham. Renew your ties with allies and others, but do not encumber yourself.

HSIEN

31 *Influence:* The time is favourable — do not put off an association or meeting. Profit immediately from the least hopeful occasion: your charm may not operate with the same vigour tomorrow.

HÊNG

32 *Duration:* You are admired and followed. This will have the happiest of consequences for you, on condition that you know how to ask relevant questions — a sometimes painful but effective operation.

TUN

33 *The retreat:* It is useless to call the masses together to announce your decisions, or to drape yourself in your resolutions — you could lose your footing.

TA CHUANG

34 *The power of the great:* Strength, movement, energy. If the tempest is favourable for you to take wing, verify the direction of the wind before taking off. Know how to make use of the currents: they can lift you to the summits, or toss you into the abyss.

CHIN

35 *Progress:* If you are offered a brilliant position as second in command, do not turn your back on it because you are aiming for a higher post. You are skilful at climbing the rungs of the ladder.

MING I

36 *The darkening of the light:* Count only on yourself; fraternity is, alas, often only a pretty word. If you are submerged in a night of solitude, tell yourself that the sun never fails to rise.

CHIA JÊN

37 *The family:* It is extremely important to you; in all circumstances and under all conditions you should think of creating a home for yourself.

K'UEI

38 *Opposition:* If you wish to have your liberty respected, think first of liberty for others. You will then see that there will be no more opposition, and you will feel free.

CHIEN

39 *Obstruction:* If the fence is too high, perhaps you can pass beneath it. The most important thing is to be clear of it. On the other hand, if you are offered a leg-up, stop digging. Do not waste your energy when help is offered.

HSIEH

40 *Deliverance:* The storm has passed. Put things in order and consolidate your ties. Give your attention to the present: each problem should be treated in due time.

SUN

41 *Decrease:* Will be hard for a Rooster who loves luxury. Put aside your ostentatious tastes and discover the beauty of wild flowers. A little self-denial may lead to plenitude.

I

42 *Increase:* Luck is with you: profit from it immediately. You are in a state of happiness. Your need for ostentatious display will be gratified to the full.

KUAI

43 *Breakthrough:* Use your authority and do not accept any sort of compromise. Be upright and control the situation; you possess everything that is needed to succeed.

KOU

44 *Coming to meet:* Do not seek to swim in troubled waters or you will lose your feathers. Turn away from still waters, but do not forget that in times of drought you will need them.

TS'UI

45 *Gathering together:* Usually it is you who rings; answer the call, even if it comes from outside.

SHÊNG

46 *Pushing upwards:* You may finally be offered a job that is worthy of you. Take care of the details, study the terrain; your success depends on your meticulousness.

K'UN

47 *Oppression:* There is nothing to worry about: a lessening of vitality does not signify a loss of your good image. Lack of self-confidence is much more dangerous than passing fatigue, and is your real enemy.

CHING

48 *The well:* Call things into question, but do not raze to the ground. Make decisions, alter and renovate — but do not uproot the foundations.

KO

49 *Revolution:* Minds are heated, the battle is imminent, but perhaps you can envisage other methods. Such seething excitement could be fatal for you.

TING

50 *The cauldron:* Symbol of the five Elements — Earth, Wood, Fire, Water and Metal. Physical and spiritual nourishment. The Rooster should both find and share the food.

CHÊN

51 *The arousing (shock, thunder):* Follow the weather forecasts carefully; large, menacing clouds which threaten to obscure the horizon are approaching. Do not change direction; you might add the dangers of the unknown to those of the storm.

KÊN

52 *Keeping still:* It is useless to struggle or to fight in a void. Stop moving about excitedly, let the hurricane pass and take refuge in solitude, which, for the moment, will be your best friend.

CHIEN

53 *Development (gradual progress):* Do not attempt to climb the rungs of the ladder four at a time, but take them as they come. Distrust your pride and your vulnerability.

KUEI MEI

54 *The bride:* Despite the favourable aspect, remain prudent and vigilant. Wait for what follows; do not be too quickly seduced by charming and sparkling appearances.

FÊNG

55 *Abundance:* Profit from it to heap up reserves. Winter will be arduous.

LÜ

56 *The wanderer:* By fixing your eyes on the horizon you know how to evaluate distances. Take the proper perspective needed for your equilibrium and for the planning of your enterprises.

SUN

57 *The gentle:* By repeating a gesture, one attains perfect ease; a quality which cannot be opposed since it does not seek opposition, but suppleness, adhesion and integration.

TUI

58 *The serene, the joyous:* Your gifts will be repaid a hundredfold. Giving will bring intense joy and unhoped for advantages.

HUAN

59 *Dissolution:* You must try, at any price, to overcome your egotism. Cease to revolt continually against the rules of the group and of the community.

CHIEH

60 *Limitation:* It is practised without violence, but is inescapable. It is a law that cannot be broken.

CHUNG FU

61 *Inner truth:* You will not be heard any better on top of a hen-house or a church, or in a public square. Evidence is not proclaimed, but witnessed in daily actions.

HSIAO KUO

62 *Preponderance of the small:* Do not waste your energy. Do not row a boat in the fog during a tempest.

CHI CHI

63 *After completion:* You are majestic and resplendent at the top of the spire, but now you must think of climbing down.

WEI CHI

64 *Before completion:* Do not sell the skin of the fox before the hunter arrives; do not descend from your tree prematurely.

General table of the years corresponding to the Chinese signs

THE RAT	THE OX	THE TIGER
31.1.1900/18.2.1901	19.2.1901/ 7.2.1902	8.2.1902/28.1.1903
18.2.1912/ 5.2.1913	6.2.1913/25.1.1914	26.1.1914/13.2.1915
5.2.1924/24.1.1925	25.1.1925/12.2.1926	13.2.1926/ 1.2.1927
24.1.1936/10.2.1937	11.2.1937/30.1.1938	31.1.1938/18.2.1939
10.2.1948/28.1.1949	29.1.1949/16.2.1950	17.2.1950/ 5.2.1951
28.1.1960/14.2.1961	15.2.1961/ 4.2.1962	5.2.1962/24.1.1963
15.2.1972/ 2.2.1973	3.2.1973/22.1.1974	23.1.1974/10.2.1975
2.2.1984/19.2.1985	20.2.1985/ 8.2.1986	9.2.1986/28.1.1987

THE RABBIT	THE DRAGON	THE SNAKE
29.1.1903/15.2.1904	16.2.1904/ 3.2.1905	4.2.1905/24.1.1906
14.2.1915/ 2.2.1916	3.2.1916/22.1.1917	23.1.1917/10.2.1918
2.2.1927/22.1.1928	23.1.1928/ 9.2.1929	10.2.1929/29.1.1930
19.2.1939/ 7.2.1940	8.2.1940/26.1.1941	27.1.1941/14.2.1942
6.2.1951/26.1.1952	27.1.1952/13.2.1953	14.2.1953/ 2.2.1954
25.1.1963/12.2.1964	13.2.1964/ 1.2.1965	2.2.1965/20.1.1966
11.2.1975/30.1.1976	31.1.1976/17.2.1977	18.2.1977/ 6.2.1978
29.1.1987/16.2.1988	17.2.1988/ 5.2.1989	6.2.1989/26.1.1990

THE HORSE	THE GOAT	THE MONKEY
25.1.1906/12.2.1907	13.2.1907/ 1.2.1908	2.2.1908/21.1.1909
11.2.1918/31.1.1919	1.2.1919/19.2.1920	20.2.1920/ 7.2.1921
30.1.1930/16.2.1931	17.2.1931/ 5.2.1932	6.2.1932/25.1.1933
15.2.1942/ 4.2.1943	5.2.1943/24.1.1944	25.1.1944/12.2.1945
3.2.1954/23.1.1955	24.1.1955/11.2.1956	12.2.1956/30.1.1957
21.1.1966/ 8.2.1967	9.2.1967/28.1.1968	29.1.1968/16.2.1969
7.2.1978/27.1.1979	28.1.1979/15.2.1980	16.2.1980/ 4.2.1981
27.1.1990/14.2.1991	15.2.1991/ 3.2.1992	4.2.1992/22.1.1993

THE ROOSTER	THE DOG	THE PIG
22.1.1909/ 9.2.1910	10.2.1910/29.1.1911	30.1.1911/17.2.1912
8.2.1921/27.1.1922	28.1.1922/15.2.1923	16.2.1923/ 4.2.1924
26.1.1933/13.2.1934	14.2.1934/ 3.2.1935	4.2.1935/23.1.1936
13.2.1945/ 1.2.1946	2.2.1946/21.1.1947	22.1.1947/ 9.2.1948
31.1.1957/15.2.1958	16.2.1958/ 7.2.1959	8.2.1959/27.1.1960
17.2.1969/ 5.2.1970	6.2.1970/26.1.1971	27.1.1971/14.2.1972
5.2.1981/24.1.1982	25.1.1982/12.2.1983	13.2.1983/ 1.2.1984
23.1.1993/ 9.2.1994	10.2.1994/30.1.1995	31.1.1995/18.2.1996

*The dates indicated specify the **first** and the **last** day of the year of the sign.*

THE HANDBOOK OF CHINESE HOROSCOPES

Theodora Lau

Are you a sentimental but crafty Rat, a serious and dutiful Ox, or a capitivating but unpredictable Tiger? Here, in the most comprehensive book ever written on Chinese astrology, you can find out which of the twelve animal signs of the lunar calendar is yours, how your sign is affected by the Yin and Yang, how your Moon sign and your Sun sign affect each other — and which of the other animal signs you're compatible with.

THE BOOK OF CHINESE BELIEFS

Frena Bloomfield

Earth magic, ghost weddings, passports to the after-life, the spirit world of the Chinese exists side-by-side with everyday reality, and affects every aspect of Chinese life from diet and decor to getting married or opening a business.

Frena Bloomfield has lived and worked in Hong Kong and has talked in depth to many practitioners of the magic arts. THE BOOK OF CHINESE BELIEFS is a fascinating introduction to a rich culture where the dead are ever-present and even the siting of a house or village is governed by the laws of earth magic.

HOROSCOPES

Arrow publish an individual Super Horoscope book for each of the twelve signs of the Zodiac, and the definitive *Handbook of Chinese Horoscopes* by Theodora Lau. These books can be bought in your local bookshop or you can order these directly by completing the form below.

SUPER HOROSCOPES 1984

____ ARIES (21 March – 20 April)	£1.50
____ TAURUS (21 April – 20 May)	£1.50
____ GEMINI (21 May – 20 June)	£1.50
____ CANCER (21 June – 20 July)	£1.50
____ LEO (21 July – 20 August)	£1.50
____ VIRGO (22 August – 22 September)	£1.50
____ LIBRA (23 September – 22 October)	£1.50
____ SCORPIO (23 October – 22 November)	£1.50
____ SAGITTARIUS (23 November – 20 December)	£1.50
____ CAPRICORN (21 December – 19 January)	£1.50
____ AQUARIUS (20 January – 18 February)	£1.50
____ PISCES (19 February – 20 March)	£1.50

Also available

____ HANDBOOK OF CHINESE HOROSCOPES	£1.95
Postage	_____
Total	_____

ARROW BOOKS, BOOKSERVICE BY POST, PO BOX 29, DOUGLAS, ISLE OF MAN

Please enclose a cheque or postal order made out to Arrow Books Limited for the amount due including 10p per book for postage and packing within the UK and 12p for overseas orders.

Please print clearly

NAME ....

ADDRESS ....

....

Whilst every effort is made to keep prices down and to keep popular books in print, Arrow Books cannot guarantee that prices will be the same as those advertised here or that books will be available.